The Amazing Animals of the Caribbean

A Journey Through the Region's Most Spectacular Wildlife

The Majestic Caribbean Flamingo

Caribbean Flamingos, known scientifically as Phoenicopterus ruber, represent the height of elegance and grace in the animal kingdom. This chapter delves deep into the complex world of these remarkable birds, detailing their unique characteristics, fascinating behaviors, and remarkable survival strategies in the Caribbean.

The Caribbean flamingo is the only flamingo species native to North America, predominantly inhabiting the Caribbean Islands and the northern part of South America. They are particularly abundant in the Bahamas, Cuba, Haiti, and the Dominican Republic. The Caribbean flamingo is the largest species of flamingo, standing impressively tall, between 120 to 140 centimeters, with a wingspan stretching up to 150 centimeters. These majestic creatures are easily recognizable by their brilliant pink or scarlet plumage, a characteristic that sets them apart from other bird species.

Flamingos are wading birds, meaning they spend a considerable amount of their time in shallow waters. They have long, thin legs and large, webbed feet, adaptations that allow them to wade into deeper waters in search of food. Their distinctively downward-bending beaks are an evolutionary marvel, designed perfectly for their unique method of filter feeding. Flamingos feed by stirring up the mud with their feet, then sucking water through their beak and filtering out small shrimp, algae, and microscopic organisms. They are equipped with a special gland that helps them remove excess salt from their bodies, a necessary adaptation for a life spent in salty waters.

One of the most intriguing aspects of the Caribbean flamingo is its vibrant color. Contrary to common belief, flamingos are not born with pink feathers. Instead, flamingo chicks hatch with a grey or white down, which gradually turns pink as they mature. The flamingo's pink hue comes from pigments called carotenoids found in their diet. Their primary food, brine shrimp and blue-green algae, are rich in these pigments, and as the flamingos digest them, the pigments get deposited in their feathers, beaks, and legs. The intensity of the pink coloration can vary based on the quality of their diet.

The Caribbean flamingos lead a highly social life. They live in colonies, sometimes numbering in the thousands. This social structure offers safety in numbers, aiding in protection from predators. It also increases their efficiency in locating food resources. They communicate through a series of vocalizations, body postures, and displays, facilitating complex social interactions.

Flamingos are monogamous birds, meaning they form long-term pair bonds. Their elaborate courtship rituals are a spectacle to behold. The process often involves synchronized group displays, where several birds engage in a sequence of stylized movements such as head-flagging, wing-saluting, and marching in unison. Once the pair forms a bond, both the male and female contribute to building a mud nest where the female lays a single large egg. Both parents take turns incubating the egg, and after about 28 to 32 days, the chick hatches. The parents diligently care for the chick, feeding it a nutrient-rich secretion known as "crop milk."

Over the years, the Caribbean flamingo population has faced several challenges. Loss of suitable wetland habitat due to human development, pollution, and climate change are significant threats. However, through conservation efforts, the population has remained relatively stable, though vigilance is required to ensure the survival of these majestic birds.

Caribbean flamingos are more than just icons of tropical elegance; they are vital components of the Caribbean ecosystem, playing essential roles in nutrient cycling and providing a rich source of food for their predators. Their continued presence serves as a testament to the resilience of nature, even in the face of human-induced pressures. Their iconic pink hue, standing tall and reflecting in the turquoise

Caribbean waters, is a sight of unparallel beauty, reminding us of the natural wonders the world holds.

In conclusion, the Caribbean flamingo, with its remarkable adaptations, fascinating life history, and incredible beauty, truly embodies the spirit of the Caribbean – vibrant, resilient, and full of life. As we move forward, it is crucial to ensure the survival of these majestic creatures, for they hold a mirror to the health of the Caribbean ecosystem and to the intertwined fate of all species on this planet.

The Enigmatic Hawksbill Sea Turtle

In the warm waters of the Caribbean, among the vibrant coral reefs and lush seagrass beds, resides a captivating marine creature with a lineage dating back over a hundred million years. This is the hawksbill sea turtle (Eretmochelys imbricata), an enigmatic species with a storied history and an uncertain future.

Hawksbill sea turtles are part of the family Cheloniidae, encompassing all the hard-shelled sea turtles. The hawksbill is distinguished from other sea turtles by its sharp, curving beak that resembles a bird's, hence the name 'hawksbill.' Moreover, its shell, or carapace, bears a pattern of overlapping scales that give it a serrated look along the edges. This distinctive pattern, combined with the shell's beautiful amber and brown hues often highlighted with streaks of gold, red, and green, makes the hawksbill sea turtle one of the most visually striking sea creatures.

Their carapace isn't just aesthetically appealing; it serves as a formidable defense mechanism against potential predators. The turtle's relatively small size, typically reaching about one meter in length and weighing between 40 and 60 kilograms, also aids its ability to swiftly navigate through the intricacies of the coral reefs, their primary habitat.

Hawksbill turtles are generally found in tropical and subtropical regions worldwide, with the Caribbean serving as one of the significant nesting sites. The warm, clear waters, abundant with coral reefs and seagrass beds, make this region an ideal habitat for these turtles. They are seldom seen in open ocean environments, preferring instead to stay near coastlines where food sources are abundant.

This species has a relatively narrow diet, predominantly consisting of sponges found in coral reef environments. They use their sharp, bird-like beaks to extract these invertebrates from crevices in the coral. This diet is unique among sea turtles and is facilitated by the hawksbill's apparent immunity to the toxins that many sponge species possess. Occasionally, they also consume jellyfish, sea anemones, and crustaceans. This diet high in calcium contributes to the growth and maintenance of their robust shell and skeletal system.

The reproductive cycle of the hawksbill sea turtle is another fascinating aspect of its biology. Female hawksbills return to their natal beaches to nest, displaying an uncanny homing instinct. Nesting season typically occurs during the summer months when females haul themselves out of the water and onto the beach to lay their eggs. A female hawksbill typically lays around 140 eggs per nest and may nest several times within a single season. The eggs incubate in the warmth of the sand for approximately two months before the hatchlings emerge and make their perilous journey to the sea.

Despite their longevity and adaptability, hawksbill sea turtles face numerous threats to their survival. They are classified as Critically Endangered by the International Union for Conservation of Nature (IUCN). Historically, they have been hunted for their shells, which are used to create decorative items, a practice commonly known as 'tortoiseshell trade.' Even though international trade in hawksbill shells is now banned under the Convention on International Trade in Endangered Species (CITES), illegal trade persists in some regions.

Moreover, habitat destruction, marine pollution, accidental capture in fishing gear, and climate change pose significant threats. Rising sea levels and increased storm activity associated with climate change may further jeopardize their nesting sites.

Efforts to conserve and protect these enigmatic creatures have been enacted worldwide, focusing on the protection of their nesting beaches, enforcement of hunting bans, and reduction of bycatch in fishing gear. Public awareness campaigns have also been instrumental in highlighting the plight of the hawksbill sea turtle and the urgent need for their protection.

In essence, the hawksbill sea turtle embodies the spirit of the Caribbean's marine environment - it is beautiful, tenacious, and full of mystery. It is a symbol of the age-old rhythm of life that unfolds beneath the waves, and a reminder of the delicate balance that exists within this vibrant ecosystem. As we strive to understand and protect the hawksbill, we are not just saving a single species but preserving a piece of our world's natural history and ensuring the continued health and vitality of our oceans.

The Endearing West Indian Manatee

Floating gently through the warm waters of the Caribbean, the West Indian manatee (Trichechus manatus) is an aquatic mammal that embodies both serenity and strength. Known for their endearing appearance and amiable disposition, these creatures invite us on an insightful journey into their remarkable world.

The West Indian manatee, also known as the American manatee, belongs to the order Sirenia, which includes three species of manatees and their cousin, the dugong. They have a large, seal-like body that tapers to a flat, paddle-shaped tail, which they use to propel themselves through the water. They have two flippers with three to four nails each, reminiscent of their distant terrestrial relatives, the elephants. Fully grown manatees are sizable creatures, typically measuring up to 4 meters in length and weighing between 400 to 550 kilograms.

Perhaps the most striking feature of the West Indian manatee is its facial expression. Their faces are broad with small eyes, and they have a pronounced snout with bristly whiskers. Their small eyes belie their sharp vision, and they use their whiskers, called vibrissae, much like cats do, to explore their environment.

Manatees are herbivores, feeding primarily on a wide variety of submerged, emergent, and floating plants. An adult manatee consumes between 4 to 9 percent of its body weight in vegetation daily, which means a 500-kilogram manatee might eat up to 45 kilograms of plants per day. However, they have been known to consume small amounts of fish and invertebrates occasionally.

West Indian manatees are slow movers, usually traveling at speeds of about 5 to 8 kilometers per hour. They are primarily solitary creatures, although they are also known to form loose aggregations in favored feeding or resting areas. Contrary to their slow and gentle demeanor, manatees are quite adept swimmers and can hold their breath for up to 15 minutes while resting. However, when they are moving, they surface every three to four minutes to breathe.

The reproductive rate of manatees is slow, which makes population recovery a challenge. Female manatees typically start breeding at around five years of age and give birth to a single calf after a year-long gestation period. Mothers and calves share a strong bond, with the calf staying with the mother for up to two years, during which time they learn essential survival skills.

West Indian manatees have no natural predators, and their primary threats are human-related. The leading causes of manatee mortality are collisions with watercraft, habitat loss, and pollution. They are sensitive to cold temperatures and require warm water habitats, which are increasingly threatened by coastal development and climate change.

Despite these challenges, concerted conservation efforts over the years have had a positive impact on manatee populations. The West Indian manatee is protected under various national and international laws and agreements, and many manatee habitats have been designated as protected areas. Additionally, public education efforts are raising awareness about the need to protect these gentle giants and their habitats.

The West Indian manatee is not just a symbol of the Caribbean's natural wealth, but also a critical indicator of its ecological health. These manatees, with their peaceful demeanor and serene presence, remind us of our fundamental connections to the natural world. They reflect the intricate interplay of life in the Caribbean waters and highlight the importance of preserving this delicate balance.

In conclusion, the story of the West Indian manatee is ultimately a story of coexistence. As we continue to learn about these extraordinary creatures and strive to protect them, we are reminded of the profound interdependence of all life forms on our planet. Their continued existence is a testament to the resilience of nature and an ongoing challenge for us to live harmoniously within our shared environment.

The Vivid Cuban Tody

On the beautiful island of Cuba, amidst a riot of vibrant flora and fauna, one small bird's brilliance outshines them all: the Cuban tody (Todus multicolor). This charming creature, adorned with an impressive palette of colors, carries the heart and soul of the Caribbean in its tiny frame.

The Cuban tody is a member of the Todidae family, an exclusive Caribbean bird family with only five known species, all of the genus Todus. However, it's the Cuban tody that holds a unique fascination due to its strikingly vibrant appearance and fascinating behavior.

This bird is compact, typically measuring just about 11 centimeters in length and weighing approximately 5 to 7 grams. What the Cuban tody lacks in size, it makes up for in color. It boasts a brilliant green upper body and wings, a snowy white underbelly, and a distinctive red throat patch. The flanks are tinged pink, and a vibrant blue streak graces each side of the face, running from the bill to just below the eye. Its broad, flat bill, essential for catching insects, is black tipped with red at the base.

The Cuban tody's habitat ranges throughout Cuba and its neighboring islands, and is impressively diverse. It can be found in forests, scrublands, and even coffee and cocoa plantations. Despite being widespread across Cuba, the Cuban tody is often hard to spot due to its small size and the fact that it's somewhat quiet, apart from its distinctive calls, which can sound like a 'tweep-tweep' or a raspy 'prrrt.'

In terms of diet, the Cuban tody is an insectivore, feeding mainly on insects and small invertebrates. It uses its wide bill to snatch its prey in swift, acrobatic flights, often returning to the same perch after catching an insect. Interestingly, before swallowing larger insects, a tody will beat the prey against a branch, possibly to stun it and remove the wings.

The nesting habits of the Cuban tody are particularly intriguing. Instead of constructing a nest in a tree or shrub, todies excavate burrows in earth banks, often alongside a road or path. Both the male and female participate in digging the tunnel, which can extend up to 45 centimeters into the bank and ends in a nesting chamber. Inside this chamber, the female lays 2 to 4 eggs, which are then incubated by both parents.

Despite its flamboyant colors, the Cuban tody faces threats that may dull its vibrant existence. Habitat loss due to deforestation and land conversion for agriculture are primary concerns. However, the Cuban tody's adaptability to different environments and its wide distribution across Cuba suggest a degree of resilience.

Efforts to conserve this incredible bird are centered around habitat preservation and management, aiming to limit deforestation and maintain the health of the ecosystems the Cuban tody calls home. Protecting this species is not just about preserving the Cuban tody itself, but also about conserving the unique biodiversity and vibrant ecosystems of the Caribbean.

In summary, the Cuban tody is a splendid representative of the Caribbean's biodiversity. Its vibrant colors mirror the rich diversity of life found in this region, and its resilience reflects the enduring spirit of Caribbean wildlife. As we delve deeper into understanding this small but remarkable bird, we're reminded of the exquisite beauty found in every corner of our planet, and of the critical importance of cherishing and protecting this diversity for generations to come.

The Ingenious Reddish Egret

The Reddish Egret (Egretta rufescens) is an exceptional bird that evokes the wild, untamed spirit of the Caribbean. Recognizable by its russet plumage and ingenious hunting technique, it is a remarkable ambassador of the region's coastal and wetland habitats.

The Reddish Egret is a medium-sized heron, standing tall at around 70-80 centimeters in height and weighing between 625-850 grams. This species is unique among herons for it comes in two distinct color morphs: dark and white. The dark morph is the most common, sporting a beautiful mixture of bluish-gray and rufous or reddish plumage, which gives the species its name. The white morph, on the other hand, is entirely white and can be mistaken for other egrets, but its two-toned bill (pink base with a black tip) and blue-gray legs set it apart.

The preferred habitats of the Reddish Egret include saltwater marshes, lagoons, mangroves, and tidal flats throughout the Caribbean, Gulf of Mexico, and the southern coast of the United States. They have a particular fondness for shallow coastal waters, where they employ their unique hunting technique.

Unlike most herons that wait patiently for fish to come within striking distance, the Reddish Egret is dynamic and theatrical in its fishing approach. This bird is known for its "canopy feeding" technique, where it uses its wings to form a canopy over its head to reduce glare and create shadow, which attracts fish. Then, with quick darting movements, it chases fish through the shallows, making it a truly entertaining spectacle to watch.

The Reddish Egret's diet consists mainly of small fish and crustaceans, and the abundance of these prey items in its habitat directly influences its breeding success. Nesting usually occurs in colonies, often with other heron species. Both males and females collaborate in building a platform nest of sticks, usually in mangroves or shrubs. Females lay 1 to 4 pale blue-green eggs, which both parents incubate for about 26 days. Chicks are cared for by both parents and fledge in about 6 to 7 weeks.

Unfortunately, this striking bird has not been immune to the pressures of habitat loss and human disturbance. Overharvesting for their beautiful plumage in the late 19th and early 20th centuries also contributed to their decline. Today, Reddish Egrets are considered a species of high conservation concern, with an estimated global population of just 7,000 breeding pairs.

Conservation efforts for the Reddish Egret focus on habitat preservation, particularly the protection of its preferred coastal and estuarine environments. Successful conservation will require continued research to understand the specific needs of this species, as well as cooperation between conservation organizations across its range.

In summary, the Reddish Egret is a testament to nature's inventiveness and adaptability. Its singular appearance and unique hunting style make it a symbol of the ecological richness and diversity of the Caribbean. As we strive to understand and protect the Reddish Egret and its habitat, we are reminded of our responsibility to coexist with nature in a manner that supports biodiversity and fosters the health of our planet's many unique ecosystems. The story of the Reddish Egret inspires us to value each species for its unique contribution to the ecological tapestry, and to strive for a future where humans and wildlife can thrive together.

The Misunderstood Caribbean Reef Shark

The Caribbean Reef Shark (Carcharhinus perezi) is one of the most common predators in the Caribbean Sea, often misunderstood and feared due to the general perception of sharks. However, this species represents a critical part of the marine ecosystem and exhibits fascinating behavior that illuminates the complex world beneath the Caribbean waves.

The Caribbean Reef Shark typically measures between 2 to 3 meters in length and weighs around 70 kilograms, making it a relatively large species. Its body is robust and streamlined, perfect for efficient swimming. It boasts a beautiful grayish-brown color on its dorsal side, blending seamlessly into the reef's colors, while its belly is a lighter, almost white color—an excellent adaptation for camouflaging in the ocean's depths.

This species is primarily found in the Caribbean Sea and the Western Atlantic, from Florida to Brazil. They prefer reef environments, where they can often be seen cruising along the outer edges of coral reefs or patrolling sandy bottoms. They're a classic example of a requiem shark, a family characterized by their migratory, live-bearing species that are often found in warm seas.

Caribbean Reef Sharks are apex predators, playing a critical role in maintaining the health of the marine ecosystem. Their diet consists mostly of bony fishes, including parrotfish, grunts, and snappers, but they're also known to eat rays, crabs, lobsters, and even other smaller shark species. This variety in their diet makes them opportunistic feeders.

Reproduction in Caribbean Reef Sharks is viviparous, meaning they give birth to live young, a trait common in many shark species. Females have a biennial reproductive cycle and give birth to 4 to 6 pups every two years. Interestingly, these sharks exhibit a behavior known as natal philopatry, where the females return to their birthplace to give birth, ensuring their offspring have a safe nursery area.

However, the Caribbean Reef Shark faces significant threats, mostly from human activities. They're often caught as bycatch in commercial fisheries but are also targeted for their meat, fins, and liver oil. The impact of recreational shark feeding activities is also a matter of ongoing debate, as it alters their natural behavior and makes them associate humans with food, potentially increasing the risk of accidents.

The species is currently listed as Near Threatened by the IUCN Red List, indicating that it could become threatened with extinction if current pressures are not mitigated. Conservation strategies for the Caribbean Reef Shark focus mainly on sustainable fishing practices, protected marine areas, and public education about the species' ecological importance.

Despite its imposing appearance and powerful predatory nature, the Caribbean Reef Shark is a creature more deserving of respect and admiration than fear. It's a crucial component of the marine ecosystem, and its survival is integral to the health and balance of the marine environments around the Caribbean.

In conclusion, the Caribbean Reef Shark epitomizes the intricacies of the Caribbean's underwater ecosystems. Its story is one of power, adaptability, and resilience, reminding us that every species, no matter how feared or misunderstood, plays a vital role in maintaining the health of our planet. As we strive to conserve and protect these magnificent creatures, we learn the true value of coexistence, understanding, and respect for all life forms.

Agile Adventurers: Caribbean Tree Frogs

When the sun sets over the Caribbean, a distinctive chorus begins to echo through the lush foliage. The symphony's conductors are small, often overlooked, yet intriguing creatures – the Caribbean Tree Frogs. This chapter introduces you to the secret life of these agile adventurers and their nocturnal escapades.

The most recognized species among these is the common coqui, or Puerto Rican Tree Frog (Eleutherodactylus coqui), named for its distinct two-part 'ko-kee' call. The coqui is more than just a frog; it is a cultural symbol for Puerto Rico. Small in stature, usually not exceeding 5 centimeters in length, the coqui compensates with its melodious voice and extraordinary adaptability.

Caribbean Tree Frogs, including the coqui, belong to the Eleutherodactylus genus, one of the most diverse anuran (frog and toad) genera. Their bodies are often brown, grey, or green, offering excellent camouflage against the leaves and bark. Remarkably, some individuals can change their body color to match their environment further.

Caribbean Tree Frogs inhabit a broad range of habitats, from wet mountain forests to semi-arid lowlands, showcasing their adaptability. However, their preferred habitats are moist and shaded environments, particularly forests and plantations.

Being nocturnal, Caribbean Tree Frogs are primarily active at night. They are insectivores, preying on a wide range of small invertebrates like spiders, mites, and insects, thus playing a crucial role in controlling the population of these organisms.

A unique aspect of Caribbean Tree Frogs, particularly the coqui, is their direct development reproductive strategy. Unlike most frogs that lay eggs in water that hatch into aquatic tadpoles, coquis lay terrestrial eggs that develop directly into small froglets. This remarkable adaptation allows them to reproduce in habitats without standing water.

However, Caribbean Tree Frogs, like many amphibians worldwide, face significant threats. Habitat loss, climate change, pollution, and disease are ongoing challenges. The deadly fungal disease, chytridiomycosis, has been a major concern for these and many other amphibian species.

Conservation strategies for Caribbean Tree Frogs focus on habitat preservation, research on their ecology and threats, and captive breeding for critically endangered species. Public awareness and education about these fascinating creatures are also crucial for their continued survival.

In conclusion, Caribbean Tree Frogs are not just another set of species in the Caribbean's rich biodiversity tapestry; they are the region's voice, filling the night with their distinctive music. They are a testament to the wonders of evolution and nature's resilience. Each tiny froglet represents hope, a new life born amidst the challenges, ready to sing its song to the moon. As we continue our journey to understand and protect these agile adventurers, we celebrate the beauty of the Caribbean's nocturnal world, a realm where every croak is a symphony, and every leaf is a stage.

The Mysterious Vampire Bat of the Caribbean

When one thinks of the Caribbean's rich biodiversity, the infamous Vampire Bat, the creature of legends and myth, inevitably springs to mind. The Common Vampire Bat (Desmodus rotundus) is a fascinating species that has adapted in unique ways to its ecological niche, embodying the mystery and intrigue of the Caribbean night.

The Common Vampire Bat is a small bat, typically weighing around 30-40 grams with a wingspan that can reach up to 40 centimeters. Its fur is short and silky, varying from dark brown to grayish in color. Its ears are large and its nose is leaf-shaped, assisting in its excellent sense of echolocation. But its most notable characteristic is its razor-sharp front teeth, which it uses to make precise cuts on its prey to lap up the blood.

Vampire Bats are found throughout the Americas, but they are particularly prevalent in the tropics, including the Caribbean islands. Their preferred habitats are warm, humid places like rainforests, swamps, and caves, where they form colonies that can number in the thousands.

Vampire Bats are the only mammals known to feed entirely on blood, a trait that has earned them their ominous name. Their victims are typically large mammals, such as cattle and horses, though they have been known to feed on birds as well. Interestingly, Vampire Bats have a highly specialized digestion system that enables them to process large volumes of blood and expel the excess water within minutes of feeding.

These bats possess a remarkable social structure, characterized by cooperative behaviors. They engage in reciprocal food sharing, where a bat that was successful in obtaining a meal will regurgitate blood to a less fortunate roost-mate. This altruistic behavior is mainly directed toward kin but can also extend to non-relatives, demonstrating complex social dynamics.

Vampire Bats reproduce once a year, usually giving birth to a single offspring. The mother bat cares for the pup, nursing it with milk for several months. Pups learn their blood-feeding behavior from their mothers, showcasing an intriguing instance of learned behavior in the animal kingdom.

Despite their ominous reputation, Vampire Bats pose little threat to humans. However, they can sometimes be carriers of diseases, such as rabies, making them a public health concern, particularly in areas where their natural habitats have been encroached upon by human activities.

The conservation status of Vampire Bats is currently of 'Least Concern' according to the IUCN Red List. Still, they are vulnerable to habitat loss and persecution due to fear and misunderstanding. Public education about the bats' ecological role is crucial to dispelling the myths that surround these fascinating creatures.

In essence, the Vampire Bat is a creature of extraordinary adaptations and complex social dynamics, embodying the mystery and intrigue of the Caribbean's nocturnal world. Their story is a testament to evolution's ability to shape life in the most unexpected ways, reminding us of the incredible diversity of life that exists in the Caribbean. As we continue to explore the unique biology and behavior of these bats, we are inspired to broaden our understanding of the natural world and our place within it, embracing the many forms of life with wonder and respect.

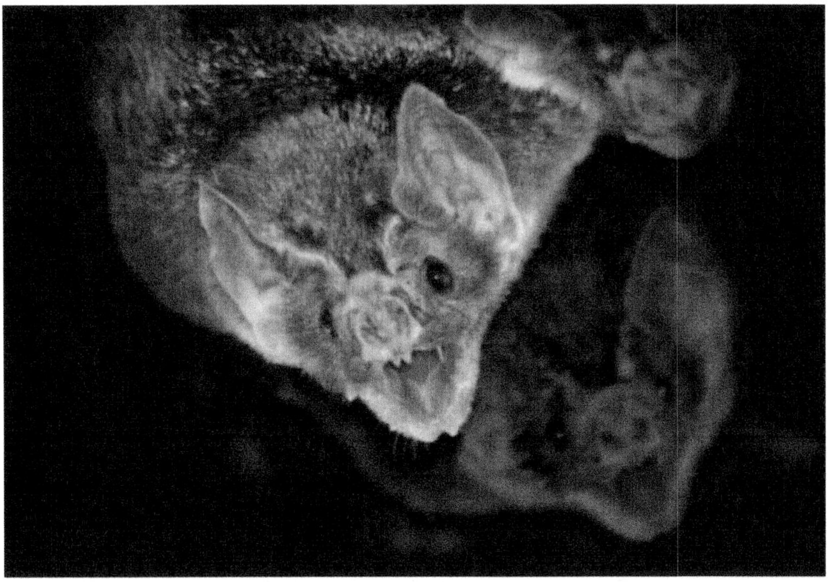

The Graceful Bluehead Wrasse

In the vibrant underwater world of the Caribbean Sea, a multitude of colors and forms dazzle the observer, but few species are as intriguing and charismatic as the Bluehead Wrasse (Thalassoma bifasciatum). This captivating fish, known for its striking coloration and fascinating life history, is an integral part of the Caribbean's marine ecosystem.

The Bluehead Wrasse is a small, slender fish that typically grows up to 20 centimeters in length. It displays a unique sexual dimorphism, which means males and females exhibit different physical characteristics. Males have a bright blue head, from which the species gets its name, along with green and yellow patterns on the body. In contrast, females and juveniles are primarily yellow with dark stripes.

The Bluehead Wrasse is found throughout the Caribbean Sea, inhabiting coral reefs and rocky substrates. They are a diurnal species, active during the day, and hiding in crevices or under corals at night.

An interesting aspect of the Bluehead Wrasse is its diet, which varies with its age and size. Smaller individuals tend to eat parasites and dead skin off other fish, a behavior known as cleaning. In doing so, they provide a vital service to the reef ecosystem by helping maintain the health of other fish species. Larger Bluehead Wrasses, on the other hand, eat a variety of invertebrates, including crabs, snails, and sea urchins.

The Bluehead Wrasse exhibits a fascinating reproductive behavior called sequential hermaphroditism. Specifically, they are protogynous hermaphrodites, meaning they begin life as females and change sex to become males later in life. This sex change is often triggered when the dominant male in a group dies, and the largest female then transforms into a male to take his place.

Bluehead Wrasses reproduce through a strategy known as broadcast spawning, where females release eggs and males release sperm into the water simultaneously. This behavior usually occurs in the early morning and is a spectacle to behold, with several males competing for the opportunity to spawn with a female.

In terms of conservation, the Bluehead Wrasse is currently listed as of 'Least Concern' by the IUCN. However, like many coral reef inhabitants, they are threatened by habitat destruction and degradation, mainly due to climate change, ocean acidification, and overfishing. Efforts to conserve and protect the vibrant coral reefs they call home are therefore crucial for their continued survival.

In conclusion, the Bluehead Wrasse is a testament to the beauty, complexity, and resilience of life in the Caribbean Sea. Their striking colors, intriguing life history, and essential role within the reef ecosystem serve as a poignant reminder of the intricate web of life that exists beneath the waves. The story of the Bluehead Wrasse calls us to marvel at the wonder of our planet's biodiversity and to recommit ourselves to the vital task of marine conservation. Through understanding and protecting species like the Bluehead Wrasse, we are preserving not just individual creatures, but the vibrant tapestry of life that they, and we, are a part of.

The Iconic Jamaican Fruit Bat

The Jamaican Fruit Bat (Artibeus jamaicensis) is an emblematic species that stands out in the rich tapestry of Caribbean wildlife. This fascinating creature, known for its vital role in seed dispersal and pollination, is integral to the health and vitality of the Caribbean ecosystems.

Typically weighing between 40-60 grams, the Jamaican Fruit Bat is a medium-sized bat with a wingspan reaching up to half a meter. It is cloaked in a fur coat that ranges from a subtle grey-brown to an almost burnt-orange hue. With its large eyes, capable of capturing even the faintest of light in the nocturnal hours, and its broad, strong wings designed for long flights, the Jamaican Fruit Bat is a creature beautifully adapted to its environment.

The Jamaican Fruit Bat is widespread throughout the Caribbean and also ranges from Mexico to Brazil in mainland regions. It thrives in a variety of habitats, including forests, swamps, and even human-dominated landscapes, roosting in caves, hollow trees, and man-made structures during the day.

As its name suggests, the Jamaican Fruit Bat primarily feeds on fruits, including figs, guava, and mangoes. The bat has a unique feeding strategy: it carries its chosen fruit to a feeding roost, devours the flesh, and then drops the seed. This behavior makes it a vital agent for seed dispersal, contributing significantly to the regeneration of plant populations. What makes the Jamaican Fruit Bat truly intriguing is its role in pollination. As it flits from tree to tree, feeding on fruits and nectar, it becomes dusted with pollen that is subsequently transferred to other flowers. This cross-pollination process is critical for the survival and diversity of many plant species.

The reproductive cycle of the Jamaican Fruit Bat usually involves birthing a single pup once or twice a year, depending on the bat's location and available food resources. Mother bats care for their young until they are ready to fly and forage independently, fostering a strong bond between mother and offspring. In terms of conservation, the Jamaican Fruit Bat has a status of 'Least Concern' on the IUCN Red List. However, it faces threats such as habitat destruction and fragmentation due to deforestation, and human disturbance in roosting sites. It is crucial to address these challenges to ensure the bat's continued survival and its ecological role in Caribbean ecosystems.

In summary, the Jamaican Fruit Bat is a fascinating creature, a winged symbol of the interconnectedness of life in the Caribbean. Its role in seed dispersal and pollination makes it an unsung hero of the region's ecological health and diversity. Through understanding and appreciating the Jamaican Fruit Bat, we can better recognize the invaluable roles even small creatures play in the greater ecological picture. The story of the Jamaican Fruit Bat inspires us to value each species, not only for their individual attributes but also for the intricate parts they play within the symphony of nature.

Master Camouflagers: Anoles of the Caribbean

Caribbean anoles, often simply referred to as 'anoles', are small, agile lizards with an uncanny ability to blend into their surroundings. These master camouflagers belong to the genus Anolis and represent a diverse group of over 150 species. This chapter will explore the remarkable characteristics, behavior, and ecological role of these captivating creatures.

Anoles exhibit a wide array of sizes, ranging from a modest few centimeters to over 20 centimeters in length. Their colors can shift between hues of green, brown, gray, and even blue, adapting to their immediate environment—a behavior that makes them virtually invisible to both predators and prey. This extraordinary ability to change color is due to specialized cells called chromatophores in their skin.

Caribbean anoles are mostly arboreal, residing in the dense foliage of trees and shrubs, but some species prefer ground or rock-dwelling habitats. They are found throughout the Caribbean islands, each species having adapted to its unique environmental niche.

The diet of anoles mainly consists of small invertebrates such as insects, spiders, and occasionally snails. Their keen eyesight and quick movements make them efficient hunters, capable of snapping up a meal within a fraction of a second.

One striking feature of anoles is their dewlap, a large flap of skin underneath their chin, which can be extended and displayed in a variety of colors. This unique characteristic is predominantly used in social and territorial displays. Males, in particular, exhibit their dewlap to assert dominance, attract females, or intimidate rivals.

Anoles display a fascinating breeding behavior. Following mating, female anoles lay a single egg, often burying it in moist soil or leaf litter. They produce several eggs over the course of a breeding season, with each egg hatching after a few weeks to reveal a miniature version of the adult anole.

Anoles play a significant role in the ecosystem as both predators and prey. They help control insect populations and, in turn, provide a food source for larger predators such as birds and snakes. Their role in the food chain, therefore, contributes to the overall balance of the ecosystem.

While most anole species are not currently endangered, they face threats such as habitat loss due to deforestation and the introduction of invasive species that compete for the same resources or prey on anoles. Efforts to conserve their habitats and control invasive species are thus crucial for their continued survival.

In conclusion, Caribbean anoles, the master camouflagers, are a testament to the incredible diversity and adaptability of life. Their vibrant displays, quick movements, and integral role in the ecosystem make them an essential part of the Caribbean's natural tapestry. The story of anoles serves as a reminder of the beauty and resilience of nature, and the necessity of preserving the delicate balance within our world's diverse ecosystems. Understanding the complex lives of anoles ultimately encourages a deeper respect for all wildlife and the crucial roles they play in maintaining our planet's health.

The Robust Rhinoceros Iguana

Among the great variety of animals in the Caribbean, the Rhinoceros Iguana (Cyclura cornuta) stands out as one of the region's most impressive reptiles. Named for the horn-like protrusions on its snout reminiscent of a rhinoceros, this robust lizard is a key component of the region's biodiversity.

Rhinoceros Iguanas are large lizards, reaching lengths up to 1.2 meters (4 feet) and weights of over 9 kilograms (20 lbs). They exhibit a grayish or greenish-brown body coloration, which assists in camouflaging them within their natural habitat. The most distinctive feature of this species is the pseudo-horn structures on their snouts, lending them their rhinoceros-like appearance.

These iguanas are primarily found on the island of Hispaniola, shared by the Dominican Republic and Haiti, although some populations exist on surrounding islands. Rhinoceros Iguanas prefer a habitat with a combination of dry forest, scrub, and rocky terrains.

One fascinating aspect of the Rhinoceros Iguana is its largely herbivorous diet. While young iguanas occasionally consume insects and small animals, adults feed predominantly on leaves, fruits, flowers, and seeds. This diet positions them as crucial seed dispersers in their ecosystem, aiding in the propagation of many plant species.

Rhinoceros Iguanas exhibit a peculiar social behavior, with males showing a strong territorial instinct. These territorial displays involve head-bobbing, inflating the body to appear larger, and if that doesn't work, physical confrontations.

These iguanas are oviparous, with females laying between 2-34 eggs once a year. The females dig burrows in sandy soil and carefully guard their nests after egg-laying, showcasing a level of maternal care uncommon among reptiles.

In terms of conservation, the Rhinoceros Iguana is classified as 'Vulnerable' by the IUCN Red List of Threatened Species. They are primarily threatened by habitat loss due to deforestation and illegal pet trade. Additionally, they face predation from introduced species such as dogs, cats, and mongoose. Efforts to conserve this fascinating creature are ongoing. These efforts include habitat protection and restoration, public education, and breeding programs. However, the plight of the Rhinoceros Iguana underscores the broader challenges facing Caribbean wildlife.

In conclusion, the Rhinoceros Iguana embodies the grandeur and resilience of Caribbean wildlife. From its distinctive pseudo-horns to its pivotal ecological role, it is a creature that commands respect and admiration. The tale of the Rhinoceros Iguana is not merely the story of a single species but a narrative of the challenges and triumphs in the preservation of our world's biodiversity. By understanding and valuing the Rhinoceros Iguana, we are one step closer to cherishing and protecting the fragile yet resilient life forms that share our planet.

The Prolific Caribbean Spiny Lobster

Caribbean Spiny Lobsters, known scientifically as Panulirus argus, are among the most prolific and recognizable marine creatures dwelling in the tropical waters of the Caribbean Sea. Known for their exquisitely patterned shells and the lack of large front claws, they are fascinating subjects in the realm of marine biology.

Caribbean Spiny Lobsters can reach lengths up to 60 centimeters (24 inches), but most individuals encountered are much smaller. They possess a multitude of spines covering their bodies, serving as a natural armor against predators. Their coloration, a combination of mottled brown, yellow, and blue hues, allows them to blend in with the seafloor, a prime example of marine camouflage. Their habitat extends throughout the tropical and subtropical waters of the western Atlantic Ocean, from Bermuda and North Carolina to Brazil. They primarily inhabit coral reefs, seagrass beds, and rocky substrates, often hiding in crevices and under ledges during the day.

The diet of the Caribbean Spiny Lobster is remarkably diverse, consisting of small invertebrates, such as crabs, mollusks, and sea urchins, as well as detritus and plant matter. They play a significant role in controlling populations of certain invertebrates, ensuring a balanced and healthy ecosystem.

One of the most intriguing aspects of the Caribbean Spiny Lobster is their gregarious behavior. These lobsters are known for their spectacular mass migrations, typically occurring in the autumn when hundreds, sometimes thousands, of individuals form single-file lines and march towards deeper waters. This behavior is believed to be a response to seasonal changes and hurricane threats. Caribbean Spiny Lobsters reproduce via external fertilization, with females carrying the fertilized eggs on their underside until they hatch into planktonic larvae. The larvae go through several developmental stages before settling onto the seafloor and metamorphosing into juvenile lobsters. The Caribbean Spiny Lobster is a crucial species for the Caribbean's fisheries and plays an essential role in the region's economy. However, this economic value makes them a target for overfishing, which is their most significant threat. Other threats include habitat loss due to coastal development and climate change, which can lead to coral reef degradation.

Conservation efforts, including fishing regulations and the establishment of marine protected areas, are in place to ensure the sustainability of lobster populations. Despite these efforts, enforcement remains a challenge, highlighting the need for enhanced management and increased public awareness about sustainable fishing practices.

In conclusion, the Caribbean Spiny Lobster, with its distinctive appearance, unique behaviors, and significant ecological and economic roles, is truly a Caribbean treasure. Understanding and appreciating these creatures promote a broader respect for marine biodiversity and the importance of sustainable practices. The story of the Caribbean Spiny Lobster is a tale of balance and interconnectivity within the marine ecosystem, serving as a reminder of our collective responsibility to safeguard our oceanic resources for future generations.

Parrotfish: Architects of the Reef

Parrotfish, the vibrant architects of the Caribbean reefs, are an indispensable part of the Caribbean's diverse marine life. With their distinct beak-like jaws, bright colorations, and pivotal role in shaping the reef environment, they are both visually and ecologically significant.

The name "parrotfish" is derived from their dental structure. They possess fused teeth that form a beak, resembling that of a parrot. This beak allows them to scrape off algae and small organisms from coral surfaces, which is a vital part of their diet.

The size of a parrotfish can vary greatly depending on the species, from the small species of just 20 centimeters (8 inches) to the larger species that can grow up to 1.2 meters (4 feet). Coloration is equally diverse, with parrotfish exhibiting a stunning array of colors and patterns. This vivid coloration serves a dual purpose: it can be used for camouflage within the colorful reef environment, and it plays a critical role in social interactions.

Parrotfish are prevalent throughout the tropical and subtropical waters of the Atlantic and Caribbean. They are primarily associated with coral reefs, which offer both abundant food and protection from predators. They have a unique method of protection: at night, some parrotfish species create a mucus cocoon around themselves, which masks their scent from potential predators.

The diet of parrotfish consists primarily of algae, which they scrape from the coral surfaces. This feeding behavior plays a crucial role in maintaining the health of the coral reefs. By removing the algae, parrotfish prevent it from overgrowing and smothering the coral. Moreover, their feeding helps to control the proliferation of seaweed, which competes with coral for sunlight and space.

While grazing on algae, parrotfish ingest coral rock, which they grind up using specialized pharyngeal teeth. The ground rock is then excreted as fine sand. A single parrotfish can produce up to a ton of sand each year, contributing significantly to the beautiful sandy beaches of the Caribbean.

Parrotfish are known for their sequential hermaphroditism. Most start life as females and change to males when they mature. This transformation is not only biological but also involves dramatic changes in color and patterns.

Parrotfish face numerous threats, primarily from overfishing and the degradation of their coral reef habitats. The loss of these "architects of the reef" has dire implications for reef health, as their role in algae control and sand production is difficult to replace.

Conservation efforts for parrotfish focus on sustainable fishing practices and the protection and restoration of coral reef habitats. These efforts are critical in maintaining the health of the reef ecosystems and the diverse array of species they support.

In conclusion, parrotfish are truly remarkable creatures. As the architects of the reef, they shape their environment in profound ways. By appreciating the roles these vibrant fish play in their ecosystems, we can begin to understand the intricate web of life that characterizes the Caribbean's coral reefs. The story of the parrotfish is a testament to the remarkable interplay of life and environment in our world's oceans.

Caribbean Hermit Crabs: Masters of Adaptation

The Caribbean hermit crab, or Coenobita clypeatus, also known as the soldier crab, the tree crab, or more endearingly as the purple pincher due to the distinctive color of one of its claws, is an engaging example of adaptability in the animal kingdom. These fascinating creatures are a common sight across the Caribbean islands, where they navigate their environment using their unique, mobile homes.

Hermit crabs are known for their characteristic behavior of living inside the abandoned shells of other animals, primarily gastropods. They do this to protect their soft, vulnerable abdomens, which lack the hard exoskeleton found on the rest of their bodies. This strategy of making use of found materials is a remarkable example of adaptation in the animal kingdom.

Caribbean hermit crabs can be distinguished from other hermit crabs by their coloration. They typically have a reddish-brown exoskeleton, and as their nickname suggests, one of their claws is usually purple, with the other being lighter or even white.

In the wild, these crabs lead a terrestrial lifestyle, unlike many other types of hermit crabs, which live primarily in the water. They are remarkably versatile, living in diverse environments ranging from sandy beaches to dense forests. These crabs are also known for their climbing skills, often found scaling vertical tree trunks in search of food or a better view of their surroundings.

The diet of Caribbean hermit crabs is as adaptable as their living arrangements. They are omnivorous scavengers, eating a varied diet that includes small animals, plant material, and carrion. This ability to eat a wide range of foods allows them to thrive in a variety of environments.

Caribbean hermit crabs exhibit fascinating social behavior, particularly during the process known as shell exchange. As they grow, these crabs need to find larger shells to inhabit. When a new shell appears, crabs will often form a sort of "queue" from largest to smallest. When the largest crab moves into the new shell, the next in line moves into the vacated shell, and so on down the line. This unique behavior is a rare example of cooperation among crustaceans.

Reproduction in Caribbean hermit crabs involves the female releasing fertilized eggs into the sea, where they hatch as larvae. These larvae undergo several stages of growth, during which they transition from a marine to a terrestrial lifestyle, and seek out their first shell.

While these crabs are not currently endangered, they face threats from habitat destruction and the pet trade. Many are captured and sold as pets each year, which can impact local populations. Education about responsible pet ownership and conservation is therefore crucial for their continued survival.

In conclusion, Caribbean hermit crabs are a testament to the power of adaptation. Their unique lifestyle, versatile diet, and cooperative behaviors have enabled them to colonize a diverse range of habitats across the Caribbean islands. These remarkable crabs are a captivating part of the region's rich biodiversity and play a vital role in their ecosystems.

The Stately Caribbean Brown Pelican

The Caribbean Brown Pelican, known scientifically as Pelecanus occidentalis, is a majestic bird that graces the coastal areas of the Caribbean Sea. Known for its unique, ample pouch and graceful flight, the Brown Pelican has a stately presence that is admired by both locals and tourists alike.

The Caribbean Brown Pelican is the smallest species among the seven species of pelicans globally. However, with an impressive wingspan that can reach over seven feet and a body length of about four feet, these birds are far from small. Brown Pelicans are distinguished by their dark brown body and white head, which becomes yellowish in older birds.

One of the most captivating features of the Caribbean Brown Pelican is its large throat pouch. This stretchy skin is used as a net to scoop up fish from the water's surface, making the Brown Pelican a specialized plunge diver. They are remarkable aviators, often seen flying in formation, low over the sea's surface, before dramatically plunging headfirst into the water to catch fish.

Caribbean Brown Pelicans primarily feed on small fish and occasionally crustaceans. They dive from as high as 65 feet to stun their prey before scooping them up in their pouch. After draining the water from their pouch, they tip back their head to swallow the fish.

Brown Pelicans breed in colonies, often on isolated islands. This colonial nesting is a strategy to protect their young from predators. Their nests are usually built in trees or shrubs but sometimes on the ground if no other options are available.

Brown Pelicans are notable for their courtship rituals. The males perform a variety of displays to attract females, such as head movements and pouch displays. After a successful courtship, the female lays two to three eggs, which both parents incubate using their webbed feet.

The chicks are born altricial, meaning they are completely dependent on their parents for food and protection. Both parents take turns feeding their young by regurgitation. After about three months, the chicks are ready to leave the nest and begin their lives independent of their parents.

The Caribbean Brown Pelican is a success story for conservation efforts. They were once threatened by the use of the pesticide DDT, which weakened the shells of their eggs and led to population declines. However, after the banning of DDT and dedicated conservation efforts, their populations have recovered significantly and they are now classified as least concern by the IUCN.

Despite this success, they still face threats from habitat loss, pollution, and disturbance of their nesting sites. Continued conservation efforts and protections are crucial to ensure the survival of these fascinating birds.

In conclusion, the Caribbean Brown Pelican is a truly stately creature, exhibiting a mix of grace and might that is rare in the animal kingdom. Their survival story is a testament to the power of conservation and serves as a beacon of hope for other species in the Caribbean. They are, undoubtedly, a highlight of the region's avian fauna.

The Flashy Caribbean King Crab

One of the most flamboyant residents of the Caribbean's underwater world is the Caribbean King Crab, also known as the Giant Red Crab or the Horse Conch. Its striking colors and large size make it a standout among the region's marine life.

The Caribbean King Crab, scientifically known as Mithrax spinosissimus, is the largest species of crab in the Caribbean Sea. It has a vibrant, red-orange shell which can span up to a foot across in adult specimens. As an inhabitant of the coral reefs, it relies on its formidable size and sturdy shell for protection against predators.

One of the most distinctive features of the Caribbean King Crab is its pair of unequal claws, each covered with a series of spikes. The larger claw is used for crushing and cutting food, while the smaller claw is used to bring food to its mouth. These crabs are omnivores, consuming a wide variety of foods, including algae, small invertebrates, and detritus.

Caribbean King Crabs are nocturnal creatures, which makes them less frequently observed by casual snorkelers or divers. During the day, they tuck themselves into crevices or under rocks. When night falls, they emerge to forage for food, using their excellent sense of smell to locate a meal.

An interesting aspect of the life cycle of the Caribbean King Crab is its growth process. Like other crustaceans, they grow by molting. As they outgrow their old exoskeleton, they shed it and produce a new one, which expands to fit their larger size before hardening. This process can occur several times during their lifetime, which can span more than ten years.

Reproduction in Caribbean King Crabs involves a courtship ritual, during which the male gently taps the female with his claws. If she is receptive, they mate, and the female later lays thousands of eggs, carrying them under her abdomen until they hatch. The hatching usually coincides with a full moon, an event that offers the larvae better chances of survival as they float with the plankton until they are big enough to settle onto the reef.

Caribbean King Crabs are an integral part of the Caribbean's marine ecosystems, playing a crucial role in controlling the populations of the creatures they consume and contributing to the overall health of the coral reefs.

Although Caribbean King Crabs are not currently listed as threatened or endangered, they face threats common to many marine species. These include habitat destruction due to coastal development and pollution, accidental capture in fishing gear, and over-collection for the aquarium trade. Conservation efforts, therefore, are essential in ensuring their survival and the continued health of the marine ecosystems they inhabit.

In conclusion, the Caribbean King Crab is a dazzling jewel of the Caribbean Sea, a testament to the region's rich biodiversity. Its striking presence adds color and intrigue to the underwater world, and its survival is intertwined with the health and diversity of the coral reefs. The story of the Caribbean King Crab is a reminder of the beauty and complexity of life beneath the waves, inspiring awe, respect, and the commitment to preserving the Caribbean's marine heritage.

The Perseverant Loggerhead Sea Turtle

The Loggerhead Sea Turtle, or Caretta caretta, is one of the most iconic residents of the Caribbean Sea. With its distinctive large head and hard shell, this turtle is a symbol of endurance and perseverance in the marine world.

Loggerheads are named for their exceptionally large heads, which support powerful jaw muscles. These jaws are capable of crushing hard-shelled prey such as conchs and whelks. Their carapace, or shell, is reddish-brown, and their plastron, or underside, is a pale yellow. Adult Loggerheads can reach up to three feet in shell length and weigh between 155 to 375 pounds.

In terms of diet, Loggerhead Sea Turtles are predominantly carnivorous, feeding on bottom-dwelling invertebrates such as crabs, mollusks, and sea urchins. However, they are also known to consume seaweed and floating sea plants, indicating an opportunistic and diverse diet.

Loggerheads are exceptional navigators, known for their long-distance migrations between feeding grounds and nesting beaches. Females return to the same beaches where they were born to lay their eggs. This homing behavior is a subject of scientific fascination, with many theories suggesting a combination of magnetic, olfactory, and celestial cues guiding the turtles' navigation.

The nesting process of Loggerheads is a sight to behold. The female hauls her large body onto the beach at night, painstakingly digs a hole using her hind flippers, and deposits around 100 to 120 eggs. She then covers the nest with sand and returns to the sea, leaving the eggs to incubate due to the heat of the sun.

After approximately two months, the eggs hatch, and the tiny turtles emerge, instinctively heading for the ocean. This is a dangerous time for hatchlings, as they are vulnerable to a variety of predators, including birds, crabs, and even fish once they reach the sea. Survival rate is low, with estimates suggesting only 1 in 1,000 hatchlings making it to adulthood.

Sadly, the Loggerhead Sea Turtle is listed as vulnerable by the International Union for Conservation of Nature (IUCN), with some populations listed as endangered. Threats to their survival include habitat loss, pollution, climate change, entanglement in fishing gear, and the illegal trade of their eggs and meat.

Conservation efforts are ongoing and multifaceted. These include protecting nesting beaches, using turtle-friendly fishing gear, and implementing sea turtle rehabilitation and rescue centers. Moreover, public education about the Loggerheads' plight and laws regulating the disturbance of nesting females and hatchlings are also crucial for the species' survival.

In conclusion, the Loggerhead Sea Turtle encapsulates the spirit of resilience and endurance, traits that enable its survival in the vast expanse of the Caribbean Sea. Its complex life cycle, fascinating behaviors, and the challenges it faces symbolize the intricacies of marine life and the pressing need for conservation efforts in our oceans. The story of the Loggerhead Sea Turtle is a testament to the richness of marine biodiversity and the intricate balance of life beneath the waves.

The Striking Bahama Oriole

In the lush landscapes of the Bahamas, a melodious song echoes through the trees, tracing its origin to the vibrantly colored Bahama Oriole. Known scientifically as Icterus northropi, this bird is a unique and fascinating member of the Icteridae family.

The Bahama Oriole is a medium-sized songbird, typically measuring around 9 inches in length. Its striking appearance sets it apart from its surroundings, with males boasting a stunning black and yellow plumage. The males have entirely black heads, backs, and wings with a contrasting bright yellow body, giving them a distinct look. Females and juveniles are slightly less vibrant, but they still retain a similar color scheme. The bird's diet is varied, including fruits, insects, and nectar, reflecting its opportunistic feeding behavior. It has a particular fondness for the fruit of the Gumbo Limbo tree and the nectar from flowers of the native Caribbean Agave plant. This varied diet contributes to its role as an important seed disperser and pollinator within its habitat.

The Bahama Oriole exhibits fascinating nesting behavior. Unlike many of its relatives who nest in open areas, the Bahama Oriole builds its nests within the protective confines of the Sabal Palm and the introduced Coconut Palm trees. The nests are woven bags, carefully created with long strips of palm leaves and thin bark. What sets the Bahama Oriole apart from many other bird species in the Caribbean is its alarming conservation status. The bird is critically endangered, with a population of less than 300 individuals estimated in the wild. This decline is primarily attributed to habitat loss due to deforestation and the introduction of the invasive Shiny Cowbird, which acts as a brood parasite, laying its eggs in the orioles' nests.

Efforts are underway to ensure the survival of this charismatic bird. Conservation initiatives are focused on habitat protection, research, and public awareness. By minimizing deforestation and managing invasive species, there is hope that the Bahama Oriole can make a resurgence. Despite the challenges it faces, the Bahama Oriole remains a symbol of the Bahamas' vibrant natural beauty. It's a testament to the delicate balance of ecosystems and the profound impact human activities can have on native species.

Listening to the melodious song of the Bahama Oriole, we are reminded of our responsibility to safeguard the fragile tapestry of life on our planet. In its melody, we hear a call to action, an appeal for conservation, and a song of resilience that echoes across the landscapes of the Bahamas. The Bahama Oriole, in its stunning contrast of yellow and black, embodies the biodiversity of the Caribbean and sings the saga of survival and perseverance. It's a story of not just a bird, but the living, breathing testament of an ecosystem's cry for help and a beacon of nature's enduring spirit.

The Effervescent Cuban Parrot

Adorned in a lavish coat of green, red, and blue, the Cuban Parrot – also known as the Cuban Amazon or by its scientific name Amazona leucocephala – graces the Caribbean skies and forests with its flamboyant charm. This parrot is not only admired for its captivating appearance but also its spirited personality, both of which we will explore in this chapter.

The Cuban Parrot stands out with its medium size, typically reaching a length of about 12 to 13 inches. Its body is primarily a vibrant green, while the edges of its feathers subtly blend into a softer, bluish-green hue, lending it an exquisite color gradient. Contrasting this verdant backdrop are patches of vibrant red on its wings and a forehead that segues from a subtle blue to white, adding a splash of color to its overall aesthetic.

An important facet of the Cuban Parrot's biology is its diet, which consists mainly of fruits, nuts, seeds, and berries. This eclectic palate plays a vital role in seed dispersal across its habitats, thereby aiding the proliferation of diverse plant species. Furthermore, their preference for certain tree species like the Royal Palm for feeding also affects their choice of nesting sites.

In terms of nesting behavior, the Cuban Parrot displays an intriguing preference for tree cavities and limestone crevices. It is known to nest in colonies, where pairs engage in a fascinating and meticulous process of preparing the nest, primarily during the breeding season, which typically falls between February and June. One fascinating aspect of their breeding behavior is their monogamous nature, with pairs often staying together for life. The Cuban Parrot, like many other parrot species, has a complex social structure. They are often observed engaging in playful behavior and interactive communication, showcasing a wide range of vocalizations that sound like melodious songs to human ears. These vocalizations are not just limited to interactions with their own kind; remarkably, the Cuban Parrot is among the group of parrot species capable of mimicking human speech. While the effervescence of the Cuban Parrot is captivating, it's crucial to address its conservation status. Classified as Near Threatened by the IUCN, the species faces threats due to habitat loss and illegal trapping for the pet trade. Protective measures are, however, being enforced to curb these issues, with education campaigns discouraging the capture and trade of these birds, and habitat preservation efforts taking center stage.

The Cuban Parrot embodies the vivacity and vibrancy of the Caribbean, symbolizing a world where nature thrives in its undisturbed form. Its charismatic presence and the melodic symphony of its calls seem to narrate a tale that transcends the boundaries of its island home, a tale that invites us to appreciate, respect, and protect the bountiful and diverse life forms that share our planet. Through their effervescent character, the Cuban Parrots tell a story of coexistence, urging us to listen, learn, and act in favor of the harmonious symphony of life.

Caribbean Lampreys: The Ocean's Vampires

Lampreys, often referred to as the 'vampires of the sea', are primitive creatures with an unusual lifestyle that has gripped the interest of many a marine biologist. Let us dive into the world of these unique, almost alien-like creatures, particularly those found in the Caribbean region, and unearth the secrets of their enigmatic existence.

Lampreys are jawless fish belonging to the order Petromyzontiformes. Unlike other fish, they possess a skeleton made of cartilage rather than bone. The most prominent and perhaps unsettling feature of lampreys is their circular, sucker-like mouth lined with rows of sharp, horn-shaped teeth. These teeth, along with a strong, piston-like tongue, are the tools of their vampiric trade, used for attaching to and feeding on the blood and bodily fluids of other fish species.

Caribbean lampreys exhibit an external morphology similar to eels, with elongated, cylindrical bodies and a single nostril on top of their heads. This streamlined body shape allows them to glide through the water with minimal resistance. They lack scales and paired fins, with their skin having a smooth, slippery texture due to the secretion of a slimy substance.

Their life cycle is as extraordinary as their appearance. Starting as larvae, known as ammocoetes, they dwell in freshwater streams for several years. These larvae are filter feeders, sifting microorganisms from the water column and the sediment. As they mature into adults, they undergo a significant metamorphosis, transforming into parasitic creatures that migrate to the sea or large lakes for their parasitic feeding stage.

Once they find a suitable host, typically a fish, they use their sucker-like mouths to attach firmly onto the body of their host. Their unique tongue then comes into play, rasping through the host's skin to access the blood and bodily fluids. Contrary to popular belief, this process does not usually kill the host fish, although it can weaken them and make them more susceptible to disease.

In terms of reproduction, lampreys, including the Caribbean species, exhibit anadromous behavior. They spawn in freshwater environments, with adults using their sucker mouths to move stones and build nests. After spawning, adult lampreys die off, leaving behind eggs that will develop into the next generation of these ocean vampires.

Conservation status and threats faced by Caribbean lampreys, as of now, are not well-studied due to a lack of comprehensive data. However, changes in water quality and the destruction of spawning grounds due to human activities pose potential threats.

While lampreys, with their 'vampiric' lifestyle, may appear to be the stuff of nightmares, they are, in reality, a crucial part of the ecosystem. Their presence indicates a healthy aquatic environment, and their larvae play an essential role in nutrient cycling. Thus, while their lifestyle may be ghastly, their ecological importance is undeniable.

In conclusion, Caribbean lampreys, though lesser-known than many other Caribbean species, offer an intriguing study into one of nature's more macabre methods of survival. This chapter gives you a glimpse of their life and ecological significance, an echo of the myriad stories hidden within the depths of the Caribbean waters. These stories, as symbolized by the lampreys, highlight the need for understanding and conserving every organism, no matter how seemingly strange or menacing, in our ever-evolving tapestry of life.

Queen Conch: The Regal Gastropod

Embodying both beauty and bounty, the Queen Conch, the subject of our current exploration, is a marvel of the Caribbean marine life. This magnificent mollusk, heralded for its ornate shell and hearty flesh, has long been an integral part of the region's ecosystem and cultural heritage.

The Queen Conch, scientifically known as Strombus gigas, is one of the largest mollusks found in the tropical waters of the Caribbean, Bermuda, and the Gulf of Mexico. This species of large sea snail boasts an impressive spiral shell, which serves as a mobile home for the creature and a symbol of the sea for many Caribbean cultures. The physical attributes of the Queen Conch are truly remarkable. Mature adults can reach up to 12 inches in length, and their shells, characterized by a glossy pink or orange interior, are coveted for their beauty. The shell's large, flared lip and tall spire, along with its overall heft and robustness, make it easily distinguishable from other marine gastropods.

The Queen Conch's diet consists mainly of algae and microscopic marine plants, which they locate using their two small tentacles. These are also used to move along the sea floor in a hopping motion, a sight that's as amusing as it is unique.

Reproduction in Queen Conchs is a captivating process. They are dioecious, meaning individuals are either male or female. Mating typically takes place during the warmer months, and the female lays thousands of tiny, transparent eggs contained in a gelatinous mass. After a few days, these eggs hatch into free-swimming larvae called 'veligers,' which eventually sink to the ocean floor and metamorphose into the adult form.

The Queen Conch's importance extends beyond its ecological role. Economically, it's a vital part of the Caribbean seafood industry, with its meat served in various culinary dishes across the region. Moreover, their shells, displaying a spectrum of warm hues, are often used in jewelry, decorative items, and even musical instruments. However, the reign of the Queen Conch is under threat. Overfishing and illegal harvesting, driven by the high demand for their meat and shells, have led to significant population decline. The degradation of their habitats, primarily seagrass beds, due to pollution and coastal development, adds another layer to their struggle for survival.

Recognizing the plight of the Queen Conch, conservation initiatives are currently in motion. Many Caribbean nations have enforced fishing regulations and seasonal closures to allow the conch population to replenish. Efforts to educate locals and tourists about sustainable practices, such as not purchasing illegal conch products, are also being implemented.

The saga of the Queen Conch is one that mirrors many challenges faced by marine species today. It underscores the delicate balance between human needs and nature's preservation. As we journey further into understanding the marvels of Caribbean fauna, let the Queen Conch serve as a reminder of our duty to safeguard our planet's incredible biodiversity.

The Distinctive Caribbean Octopus

Dive into the enchanting underwater world of the Caribbean and you'll encounter a fascinating resident - the Caribbean octopus, known scientifically as Octopus briareus. This master of camouflage and escape artistry offers us a captivating example of adaptation and survival beneath the waves.

Octopus briareus is most recognizable for its long, slender arms adorned with two rows of suckers. With an average arm span of three feet, the Caribbean octopus is not the largest of its kind, but it's certainly one of the most intriguing. This species' body color is usually brownish-red, but it can quickly shift hues thanks to specialized cells in its skin known as chromatophores.

The Caribbean octopus is a nocturnal creature, hiding in rocky crevices during the day and emerging at night to hunt for a variety of prey, including crabs, shrimp, and various types of mollusks. The octopus ensnares its victims with its arms, pulling them into reach of its hard beak – the only rigid part of its body – to deliver a fatal bite.

Their hunting prowess isn't their only noteworthy characteristic. In fact, the true marvel of the Caribbean octopus lies in its incredible ability to adapt its appearance to its surroundings. Utilizing chromatophores and specialized muscles, it can alter the color, pattern, and even texture of its skin to mimic a wide array of objects, from coral and rocks to sand and seaweed. This chameleon-like ability is primarily used to elude predators and ambush prey.

In terms of reproduction, the life cycle of the Caribbean octopus is a poignant narrative of life and death. Mating involves the male inserting a specialized arm called a hectocotylus into the female's mantle cavity to deposit spermatophores. After mating, the male's lifecycle comes to an end, while the female lives just long enough to guard her eggs, ceasing to eat and ultimately passing away after they hatch.

Caribbean octopuses also demonstrate a remarkable intelligence that sets them apart from most other invertebrates. They've been known to use tools, navigate mazes in laboratory settings, and even unscrew lids to obtain food, reflecting problem-solving capabilities that hint at a complex inner life.

Despite their intelligence and adaptability, Caribbean octopuses are not without threats. Overfishing and habitat destruction caused by pollution and climate change-induced coral bleaching are significant challenges to their survival. Furthermore, they are often caught as bycatch in fishing nets, contributing to population declines.

Conservation efforts for Caribbean octopuses primarily revolve around protecting their habitat. Establishing marine protected areas, promoting sustainable fishing practices, and reducing water pollution are key strategies to ensure the survival of this remarkable species.

In closing, the Caribbean octopus offers a lens into the wonders of the marine world, showcasing evolution's handiwork in its striking adaptability, problem-solving intelligence, and poignant lifecycle. A symbol of the ocean's mystery and an emblem of adaptability, it represents the extraordinary life that calls the Caribbean Sea home.

The Intimidating Barracuda

If one were to take a journey beneath the sparkling surface of the Caribbean Sea, it wouldn't be long before encountering one of its most formidable denizens - the Barracuda. Known for their torpedo-shaped bodies, fearsome appearance, and quick bursts of speed, barracudas hold a unique position in the tropical marine ecosystem.

The Great Barracuda, scientifically known as Sphyraena barracuda, is the species most commonly found in the Caribbean. These impressive fish can reach lengths of up to 6 feet and are immediately recognizable by their long, slim bodies, silver scales, and prominent, razor-sharp teeth, which are capable of piercing even the toughest of fish skins.

Barracudas are ambush predators, relying on their excellent eyesight and extraordinary speed to capture their prey. They're known to feed on a wide variety of fish, including mullets, groupers, and even smaller members of their own species. With a burst speed that can reach up to 27 miles per hour, few creatures can escape a barracuda's strike when within its sights.

One of the most intriguing aspects of the barracuda's behavior is its hunting strategy. Often, they remain motionless in the water or slowly cruise the sea floor, blending in with their surroundings until an unsuspecting fish passes by. In a lightning-fast strike, the barracuda snatches its meal, returning to its lurk-and-wait tactic for the next opportunity.

In terms of reproduction, barracudas are broadcast spawners. This means that females release their eggs into the water, where they are fertilized by males. The eggs then drift with the ocean currents, hatching into larvae that eventually grow into juvenile barracudas. This reproductive strategy, while common among many fish species, makes the young particularly vulnerable to predation and changing environmental conditions.

Despite their fearsome reputation, barracudas are not typically a threat to humans unless provoked. While there have been instances of barracudas biting divers and swimmers, such incidents are rare and usually a result of mistaken identity or defensive behavior. However, the size and speed of the barracuda command respect and caution.

Barracudas, like many marine species, face challenges due to human activity. Overfishing, pollution, and habitat degradation threaten their populations. Moreover, they are also susceptible to ciguatera poisoning, a disease caused by consuming fish that have ingested toxic marine microalgae. This not only affects the barracudas but also humans who consume infected fish.

Conservation efforts for barracudas focus on implementing sustainable fishing practices, enforcing fishing regulations, and creating marine protected areas. Public education is also a significant component of these efforts, as raising awareness about the importance of barracudas in marine ecosystems can encourage practices that contribute to their conservation.

In conclusion, the barracuda is an iconic figure within the Caribbean marine world. As efficient predators, they play a crucial role in maintaining the health and balance of the ecosystem. With their glimmering silver bodies and impressive speed, they add a sense of awe and respect to the incredible diversity of life beneath the Caribbean waves.

The Pioneering American Crocodile

Silhouetted against the sunset, a long, reptilian figure skims the water's surface with a grace that belies its immense size. This is the American crocodile, an iconic species of the Caribbean and a beacon of resilience and adaptation. They are a living testament to the ancient lineage of reptiles, predating even the dinosaurs.

The American crocodile (Crocodylus acutus) is one of the most prominent crocodile species found throughout the Caribbean, southern Florida, and parts of Central and South America. They inhabit coastal areas, freshwater habitats, and brackish waters—a testament to their adaptability.

Characterized by their narrow, V-shaped snouts, American crocodiles boast a body armored with sturdy, raised scales, known as scutes, providing a natural shield against predators. They are among the larger crocodile species, with males reaching lengths of up to 20 feet and females being slightly smaller.

Their coloration is generally grayish-green, which allows them to blend seamlessly with their surroundings. However, perhaps the most fascinating physical aspect of these crocodiles is their eyes. Like all crocodilians, they possess a tapetum lucidum, a layer of cells in the back of the eye that reflects light back through the retina, significantly enhancing their night vision. This feature, paired with their ability to close their nostrils and ears when submerged, makes them formidable hunters both day and night.

The American crocodile's diet is as varied as its habitat, consuming everything from fish and crustaceans to small mammals and birds. Their impressive, conical teeth are designed not for chewing but for gripping and tearing. The crocodile's famous "death roll" is a method used to break off digestible pieces from larger prey.

However, this powerful predator exhibits a gentler side during reproduction. Both sexes show considerable parental care, with females meticulously guarding their nests and, after the eggs hatch, carrying their young in their mouths to the water—a stark contrast to their reputation as fierce predators.

Sadly, the American crocodile population faces considerable threats, with habitat loss due to coastal development being a primary concern. Pollution and human-wildlife conflict also pose significant challenges to their survival. Despite these adversities, they are protected by legislation in many areas where they reside, and conservation efforts, such as habitat preservation, are in place.

American crocodiles are also a key species for maintaining the health of their ecosystems. As apex predators, they help control the populations of certain species, contributing to a balanced ecosystem. In addition, their nests promote vegetation growth by aerating the soil.

The American crocodile is a creature of contrasts: a powerful predator with a tender touch toward its offspring; a resilient survivor amidst mounting threats; a vital cog in the ecosystem machine. They serve as a vivid reminder of the intricate and often paradoxical beauty of nature, embodying the pioneering spirit that underpins the diverse wildlife of the Caribbean. As such, their survival is not just a matter of species conservation, but a critical element in preserving the integrity and balance of their habitats. As we move forward, understanding and protecting these remarkable creatures is of paramount importance, ensuring that future generations can marvel at the pioneering American crocodile.

The Dashing Caribbean Spiny-tailed Iguana

As the Caribbean sun bathes the rocky shores in its warm glow, a distinctive creature emerges from its crevice - a creature covered in scales, its tail studded with spines. This is the Caribbean Spiny-tailed Iguana, a reptile whose unique appearance and habits embody the richness of the Caribbean biodiversity.

The Caribbean Spiny-tailed Iguana (Genus Ctenosaura), also known as the Black Iguana or Wish Willy, is a species of lizard native to the arid landscapes of the Caribbean islands, as well as Central America. Characterized by its spiny tail from which it derives its name, this creature is an important part of the local ecosystem.

Typically medium to large in size, the Caribbean Spiny-tailed Iguana boasts a remarkable physical appearance. Its body, painted in a palette of grays, creams, and blacks, serves as an excellent camouflage against the rocky terrain. The iguana's most distinctive feature, the spiny tail, is a formidable defense mechanism against predators.

Their diet is mainly herbivorous, comprising of flowers, leaves, stems, and fruit, but they can also adapt to an omnivorous diet if necessary, occasionally consuming small animals and eggs. This dietary adaptability is a key factor in their survival in varied environments.

Caribbean Spiny-tailed Iguanas are known for their remarkable agility and speed. They are excellent climbers, often found basking on branches, rocks, and even rooftops. When threatened, they can swiftly escape by running to their burrows or climbing trees, leaving predators dazed and confused.

Breeding season for these iguanas typically falls between February and March, with females laying clutches of five to twenty eggs in burrows. The young iguanas hatch after about ninety days, already equipped with the skills to climb and hide for survival.

Yet, the journey of the Caribbean Spiny-tailed Iguana is not without challenges. They face threats from habitat loss, invasive species, and hunting for meat and the pet trade. In some areas, they are considered pests due to their appetite for agricultural crops.

Despite the hurdles, the Caribbean Spiny-tailed Iguana displays a commendable resilience. Their adaptability, from diet to environment, coupled with protective legislation and conservation efforts, has seen populations sustain themselves, even flourish, in some parts of their range.

The Caribbean Spiny-tailed Iguana serves as a symbol of the rich and varied biodiversity of the Caribbean. Their story reminds us of the intricate balance of nature and the importance of each species in an ecosystem. The spiny-tailed iguana, with its unique traits and survival story, adds a distinct shade to the vibrant tapestry of Caribbean wildlife.

As we bask in the Caribbean sun, let us remember the Spiny-tailed Iguana, whose story of survival resonates within the rocky crevices it calls home. The sun casts long shadows of these resilient creatures, underscoring their continued existence and the importance of our shared responsibility towards their preservation.

Nurse Sharks: The Gentle Giants

In the blue realm beneath the waves, among a kaleidoscope of tropical fish and corals, a formidable figure glides through the water. With a body that speaks of strength and resilience, the Nurse Shark, one of the gentle giants of the Caribbean, silently patrols the ocean floor.

Nurse Sharks (Ginglymostoma cirratum) are a species of bottom-dwelling sharks known for their docile nature and distinct physical features. Their skin varies from tan to dark brown, providing excellent camouflage against the sandy seafloor. They possess a broad, flat head and small eyes, and their mouths are located on the underside of their bodies, housing thousands of tiny, serrated teeth. Perhaps the most unique characteristic is the pair of sensory organs, known as barbels, hanging from their upper lip, aiding them in locating prey in the sandy substrate.

Unlike many of their kin, Nurse Sharks are not agile, swift swimmers. Instead, they are sluggish, often found resting during the day in large groups on the ocean floor, tucked under rocky ledges or within crevices in the reef. However, as night falls, these gentle giants become solitary hunters, scouring the seabed for food.

Their diet predominantly consists of small fish, sea urchins, crustaceans, and mollusks, which they suck into their powerful jaws with a surprising speed. Nurse Sharks are also known to dig into the sandy bottom with their snouts to unearth hidden prey, a testament to their adaptability and resourcefulness.

In terms of reproduction, Nurse Sharks are ovoviviparous, a method where the eggs hatch within the female's body, and the pups are born live. The gestation period lasts around six months, after which the female gives birth to a litter of 20 to 30 pups.

Despite their intimidating size, reaching lengths up to 14 feet, Nurse Sharks are generally harmless to humans unless provoked. Their gentle nature has made them popular among divers and snorkelers, serving as ambassadors for their species, and challenging the stereotype that all sharks are dangerous.

However, Nurse Sharks are not without threats. While they have few natural predators, human activities pose significant challenges. Overfishing, both for their meat and the aquarium trade, coupled with habitat degradation, has put their populations under stress.

Efforts are being made for their conservation. Certain regions have placed restrictions on fishing and trade of Nurse Sharks, while others have established marine protected areas, safeguarding their natural habitats. Education about their importance in the ecosystem also plays a critical role in their protection.

In the grand tapestry of Caribbean marine life, Nurse Sharks are integral threads. Their presence is a testament to the ocean's diversity and the delicate balance of life it harbors. As we dive into the blue depths and encounter these gentle giants, let us be reminded of our duty to protect these majestic creatures and the marine environment they inhabit.

As the sun's rays filter through the turquoise waters, illuminating the quiet, sandy bottom, the Nurse Shark continues its graceful journey – a gentle giant living in harmony with its surroundings, contributing to the ocean's rhythm and playing its part in the fascinating tale of the Caribbean Sea.

Caribbean Sea Stars: Sunbursts of the Sea

In the Caribbean's rich tapestry of marine life, sea stars, or starfish, hold a unique allure. Known for their iconic star-shaped silhouette, they are a prominent part of the underwater landscape, adding to the area's vibrant biodiversity.

Sea stars belong to the class Asteroidea, within the phylum Echinodermata, which also includes sea urchins, sand dollars, and sea cucumbers. They possess a distinct radial symmetry with arms, or rays, that extend from a central disk. This layout is a fundamental feature, leading them to be fittingly named 'starfish'.

One of the most widely recognized Caribbean sea stars is the Cushion Sea Star (Oreaster reticulatus), known for its large size, broad central disc, and short, rounded arms. They come in a variety of colors, from red and orange to brown and tan, and they typically grow to around 20 cm in diameter, though larger specimens have been found.

The underside of the sea star contains its mouth and hundreds of tiny tube feet arranged in a groove along each arm. These tube feet, filled with sea water, allow the sea star to move slowly but effectively across the seafloor. Additionally, they serve as sensors and even assist the sea star in feeding by helping to open shells of their prey.

When it comes to diet, Caribbean Sea Stars are largely omnivorous and exhibit two types of feeding behavior: predation and scavenging. They feed on a variety of food sources, including mollusks, small crustaceans, detritus, and even dead fish. Interestingly, they have the ability to eject their stomach out of their body to envelop and digest their prey, allowing them to consume food larger than their mouth.

Sea stars play an important role in maintaining balance within their ecosystems. They help control the populations of various marine organisms and contribute to the decomposition process by feeding on dead matter.

In terms of reproduction, sea stars have a rather fascinating ability: regeneration. They can regrow parts of their bodies, and some species can even regenerate an entirely new sea star from just a portion of a severed limb. This remarkable capacity helps sea stars recover from injuries and contributes to their resilience as a species.

Despite their fascinating characteristics and significant role in marine ecosystems, Caribbean Sea Stars face several challenges. Human activities, including coastal development, pollution, and climate change, contribute to the degradation of their habitats. Moreover, sea stars are often collected for the aquarium trade or as souvenirs, which can negatively impact local populations.

Efforts are being made to protect and conserve these marine invertebrates. Marine Protected Areas (MPAs) and legislation limiting collection can help safeguard their populations. Additionally, public education about the ecological importance of sea stars and the threats they face is crucial.

As we explore the vibrant seafloors of the Caribbean and come across these sunbursts of the sea, it's crucial to recognize our role in preserving their habitats. Through understanding and respect, we can ensure that these magnificent creatures continue to thrive and bring beauty to the Caribbean Sea for generations to come. Caribbean Sea Stars, with their radiant presence and ecological importance, truly symbolize the richness and resilience of the marine world.

The Cryptic Caribbean Ghost Crab

As our exploration of Caribbean fauna continues, let's turn our gaze from the vibrant seafloor to the fascinating shores where land and sea intertwine. Here, the elusive and captivating Ghost Crab makes its home. These creatures are an integral part of the coastal ecosystem, embodying the unique character of the Caribbean's sandy habitats.

The Ghost Crab, scientifically known as Ocypode quadrata, derives its common name from its uncanny ability to disappear from sight, blending seamlessly with its sandy environment. This crustacean is an undeniable master of camouflage, making it a captivating subject of study.

Ghost crabs display significant adaptability, inhabiting various environments from dunes to mangroves. They are primarily nocturnal, which contributes to their elusive reputation. During the day, they retreat into their burrows, tunnels dug into sand or soil, which provide protection from predators and harsh weather, as well as help to regulate their body temperature.

Physically, Ghost Crabs possess a set of fascinating features that equip them for survival in their environment. They have a square-shaped, semi-translucent body, with colors ranging from sandy yellow to pale gray, and even a pinkish hue – all depending on their specific habitat. Their two large eyes, set on stalks, can rotate 360 degrees, providing a panoramic view of their surroundings. This exceptional visual acuity aids in spotting potential threats and locating food.

Another distinguishing feature is their asymmetric claws, with one larger than the other. The larger claw, often waved in a signaling manner, serves multiple functions: from asserting dominance and attracting mates to defense and feeding. The smaller claw, on the other hand, assists in more delicate tasks such as grooming and handling food.

The diet of Ghost Crabs is diverse and largely opportunistic. They feed on a variety of plant and animal material, including algae, insects, mollusks, and detritus. Occasionally, they might even resort to cannibalism, particularly in situations of high population density or limited food resources.

Ghost Crabs are primarily terrestrial but remain closely tied to the ocean. They require saltwater for survival, and female Ghost Crabs release their eggs into the sea, where the larvae develop before returning to land as juvenile crabs. This life cycle underscores the intricate link between land and sea embodied by these crabs and the importance of conserving both habitats.

Despite their resilience and adaptability, Ghost Crabs face several threats. Coastal development and beach tourism can lead to habitat loss and disturbance. Pollution, especially plastic waste, poses another major concern, often leading to entanglement or ingestion.

Efforts to conserve these cryptic creatures involve protecting their habitats and mitigating human-induced disturbances. Regulations for beachfront construction, beach clean-ups, and education about the importance of these crabs can help ensure their continued survival.

Ghost Crabs, with their cryptic charm and essential role in the coastal ecosystem, symbolize the often-overlooked, yet incredibly diverse life that flourishes at the fringes of land and sea. As we stroll the beaches of the Caribbean, let's remember to tread lightly and respect the unseen life that makes these places truly magical.

The Ingenious Smooth Trunkfish

As we delve deeper into the mesmerizing world of Caribbean marine life, we find ourselves captivated by the unique and charming Smooth Trunkfish. As part of the family Ostraciidae, it's one of the many fascinating species that enliven the waters of the Caribbean, displaying a host of ingenious adaptations that serve as compelling proof of the complexities of evolution.

The Smooth Trunkfish, or Lactophrys triqueter, as it is known in scientific circles, is not a typical fish in the conventional sense. Its exterior boasts a hard, bony surface that resembles a carapace, an evolutionary innovation providing excellent protection against predators. The body is predominantly black, with a sprinkling of white spots, which grants it a distinctive, starry appearance, while its angular, box-like shape offers a stark contrast to the common streamlined silhouette of many fish species.

One of the defining features of the Smooth Trunkfish is its mode of locomotion. Instead of swimming in a lateral motion like most fishes, the Trunkfish uses a unique method of propulsion. Its pectoral fins flutter rapidly, propelling it through the water with an amusing, yet surprisingly effective, bumblebee-like movement. This peculiar form of locomotion, coupled with its sturdy carapace, gives the Smooth Trunkfish an incredible degree of maneuverability, allowing it to navigate the coral reefs' intricate maze with ease.

The size of an adult Smooth Trunkfish ranges from six to twelve inches, with females often being larger than males. They possess puckered, tubular mouths, a trait that is particularly advantageous for their feeding habits. Primarily benthic feeders, they use their small mouths to blow jets of water into the sandy sea floor, exposing hidden prey such as mollusks, crustaceans, and small fish. This unique feeding behavior showcases the Smooth Trunkfish's remarkable adaptability and resourcefulness.

In terms of social behavior, Smooth Trunkfish display interesting dynamics. They are solitary for most of their lives, but during the mating season, males court females with a curious dance. Once the female has laid her eggs, the male will fertilize them, and the parents leave the eggs to develop and hatch on their own, a common strategy among many fish species. Smooth Trunkfish, while resilient, are not without threats. Their primary predators are larger fish species and sea birds. However, the Smooth Trunkfish's bony carapace and ability to release a toxin when threatened provide it with robust defense mechanisms. Human-induced changes such as ocean pollution, habitat destruction, and climate change pose significant threats, underscoring the importance of sustainable practices and conservation efforts.

The Smooth Trunkfish, with its endearing appearance, resourceful feeding habits, and intriguing locomotion, is a testament to the staggering biodiversity that graces the Caribbean waters. As we marvel at the vibrant spectacle of the Caribbean seascape, we must remember our role in ensuring that future generations have the opportunity to be entranced by the ingenious Smooth Trunkfish.

The Threatened Jamaican Iguana

The Caribbean archipelago is replete with a myriad of captivating wildlife, each species possessing its unique charm and intriguing ecological role. However, few creatures illustrate the beauty, resilience, and vulnerability of Caribbean fauna quite like the Jamaican Iguana, Cyclura collei.

The Jamaican Iguana, often mistaken for a lizard, is, in fact, a large herbivorous reptile. Its impressive body stretches up to nearly five feet in length, with males typically larger than females. Clad in a somber palette of greys and greens, this reptile is equipped with a row of spines running from the nape of its neck to the tip of its tail, lending it a prehistoric, dinosaur-like appearance.

Their preferred habitats are the dry forests of limestone hills, with the Hellshire Hills in St. Catherine, Jamaica, being one of their last known strongholds. These creatures are primarily diurnal, active during the day and resting during the night. They spend their active hours foraging for leaves, flowers, and fruits, although they may occasionally snack on invertebrates, a testament to their opportunistic dietary habits.

The Jamaican Iguana showcases an interesting aspect of its reproductive biology. Females lay their eggs in sunny, sandy areas, often returning to the same nesting sites year after year. After a gestation period of approximately 85 days, hatchlings emerge from the eggs, beginning their perilous journey of survival.

While these facts illuminate the intriguing lifestyle of the Jamaican Iguana, it is their conservation status that truly underscores the delicate balance of biodiversity in the Caribbean. In the mid-20th century, the Jamaican Iguana was feared to be extinct, with no sightings for several decades due to habitat destruction, hunting, and predation by invasive species. It was only in 1990 that a single male was accidentally discovered, sparking renewed hope for the species.

The subsequent launch of the Jamaican Iguana Recovery Program has facilitated valuable research and protective measures, resulting in a slow, but steady increase in the iguana population. Yet, the challenges remain formidable. Habitat destruction, primarily due to deforestation for development and agriculture, continues to threaten their survival. Invasive predators like mongooses, cats, and dogs pose a significant danger, particularly to hatchlings.

The story of the Jamaican Iguana is a poignant reminder of the fragile nature of biodiversity. It demonstrates how each species, no matter how obscure or seemingly unimportant, plays an essential role in maintaining ecological balance. It also underscores the vital importance of conservation efforts, not only for the survival of individual species but for the health of our global ecosystem.

The Jamaican Iguana, resilient yet threatened, remains a beacon of hope. It's a testament to nature's tenacity and the power of concerted conservation efforts. As we continue to explore the wonders of the Caribbean, we are reminded of our responsibility - to appreciate, protect, and preserve these diverse, vibrant ecosystems for generations to come.

The Gallant Crested Caracara

As we delve into the heart of the Caribbean, we encounter a striking resident of the avian world - the Crested Caracara, a bird that embodies both ferocity and grace. Known scientifically as Caracara cheriway, this bird of prey holds an aura of majesty that is befitting of its status within the bird kingdom.

The Crested Caracara is a member of the Falconidae family, albeit quite unorthodox in comparison to its swift, airborne cousins. It flaunts a powerful build, standing tall with a body length reaching 23 inches and a wingspan spreading up to approximately 50 inches. Adorned with a black and white body, the Crested Caracara boasts a striking contrast that is easily recognizable. Its signature characteristic, the black crest on its head, adds a regal touch to its overall appearance.

Their habitat spans from Florida, Mexico to northern parts of South America, including the Caribbean, where they favor open lands such as prairies and savannas. Despite their ability to fly, Crested Caracaras are often found on the ground, strutting with an authoritative gait that echoes their dominant status.

Contrary to most falcons who are exclusive carnivores, the Crested Caracaras display a more adaptable, opportunistic feeding behavior. While they readily prey on small mammals, birds, and reptiles, they're also known scavengers, frequently seen at carrion sites. This dietary versatility is key to their survival in diverse habitats.

In terms of reproduction, the Crested Caracara follows a monogamous breeding system, with pairs often mating for life. These birds nest in trees, shrubs, or even on the ground, lining their nests with leaves, sticks, and cow dung, an unusual habit thought to deter predators. They lay up to three eggs, which both parents incubate diligently.

The Crested Caracara is not only an impressive sight but also plays a crucial role in the ecosystem. As scavengers, they contribute significantly to the natural process of decomposition and nutrient recycling. Yet, like many of their fellow Caribbean creatures, they face the harsh realities of habitat loss, primarily due to land development and agriculture expansion.

However, the resilience of the Crested Caracara, coupled with their adaptive feeding behavior, allows them to maintain a stable population. They're classified as 'Least Concern' by the International Union for Conservation of Nature (IUCN), indicating their current security as a species. Nonetheless, continual monitoring and habitat preservation efforts are essential to ensure their future.

The Crested Caracara is a testament to nature's incredible diversity and adaptability. Their unique characteristics and ecological importance underline the significance of each creature in the intricate tapestry of life. As we marvel at the gallant Crested Caracara, we are reminded of our collective responsibility to protect and nurture these precious ecosystems for generations to come. As we continue our journey across the vibrant Caribbean, we carry with us an even greater appreciation of its wildlife and an unwavering commitment to its conservation.

The Marvelous Mangrove Cuckoo

In the lush green tapestry of the Caribbean Mangroves, an elusive bird dwells, capturing the hearts of birdwatchers and nature lovers alike - the Mangrove Cuckoo, scientifically known as Coccyzus minor. This extraordinary bird with its distinctive calls is a symbol of the health and vitality of the mangrove ecosystems it inhabits.

Physically, the Mangrove Cuckoo is a sight to behold. They typically measure between 11 and 12 inches in length, and their plumage exhibits a charming contrast of colors. A dusty gray-brown coat adorns their upper body, while the underparts boast a glorious yellow. The bird's black mask and long, curved bill lend an air of mystery, making them one of the mangrove's most intriguing residents.

Native to the tropics of the New World, the Mangrove Cuckoo has a wide distribution. In the Caribbean, they're found throughout the Greater Antilles and the Bahamas, favoring mangrove swamps, coastal hammocks, and scrublands. Their preferred habitats are typically near water bodies, accentuating their affinity for the tranquility of coastal ecosystems.

The Mangrove Cuckoo is a skilled forager, predominantly feeding on insects and caterpillars. They're also known to incorporate small lizards, fruits, and berries into their diet, an adaptive trait that serves them well in their diverse habitats.

Despite being common within their habitat range, the Mangrove Cuckoos are infamously elusive, often staying well-hidden among the foliage. Their unique, mournful calls, however, often give away their presence to the keen ear. This enigmatic behavior has made them a sought-after sighting among bird enthusiasts.

Breeding between March and July, the Mangrove Cuckoo's nest is a modest structure, usually a shallow cup of twigs and leaves tucked within dense foliage. It lays two to three eggs, which are incubated by both parents. The young are altricial, meaning they are born helpless and rely on parental care for survival in the initial stages of their life.

The Mangrove Cuckoo's status as per the International Union for Conservation of Nature (IUCN) is 'Least Concern', largely due to their extensive range. However, they are not immune to the broader environmental threats affecting their habitat, such as coastal development, pollution, and climate change.

Mangrove Cuckoos play a vital role in their ecosystem, controlling insect populations and dispersing seeds through their frugivorous tendencies. Their presence, therefore, is often a good indicator of a healthy mangrove ecosystem, serving as a symbol for conservation efforts in these habitats.

The tale of the Mangrove Cuckoo serves as a compelling narrative about the wonders hidden within the Caribbean mangroves. It reminds us of the intricate relationships between species and their habitats, reinforcing the importance of preserving these unique ecosystems for the myriad life forms they support. As we journey further into the rich tapestry of Caribbean wildlife, let's carry the story of the Mangrove Cuckoo as a testament to nature's resilient and marvelous creations.

The Curious Nassau Grouper

In the grand theatre of the Caribbean Sea, where myriad marine creatures steal the limelight, the Nassau Grouper, known scientifically as Epinephelus striatus, holds a unique standing. This intriguing fish, recognized by its distinctive features and interesting behavior, has fascinated marine biologists and underwater explorers alike.

In terms of appearance, the Nassau Grouper is indeed striking. Measuring up to four feet and weighing around 55 pounds, it's a robust creature. Its body exhibits a tan or light background color, interspersed with five darker brown vertical bars, and a distinctive black tuning-fork pattern adorns the top of its head, providing a simple means of identification.

One characteristic feature of the Nassau Grouper is its ability to change color patterns. Depending on its mood, surroundings, or during spawning, the grouper may transform into a bicolor pattern, where the back and upper side of the body turns dark, and the lower side stays light. This chameleon-like trait makes it one of the most visually intriguing inhabitants of its marine habitat.

Native to the coastal waters of the western Atlantic Ocean, the Nassau Grouper is primarily found in the Bahamas and the Caribbean Sea. They inhabit rocky and coral reefs, showing a preference for shallow waters, although they are known to venture into depths reaching 130 feet.

The Nassau Grouper's diet primarily consists of fish and small crustaceans, and it's a formidable hunter. Using an ambush strategy, the grouper remains motionless and blends with its surroundings, waiting for unsuspecting prey to come within striking distance. Then, it opens its large mouth and dilates its gills to create a powerful suction to draw in the prey, a hunting technique that is as efficient as it is fascinating.

The social structure of the Nassau Grouper is notably captivating. Unlike most groupers, which are solitary, the Nassau Grouper occasionally forms large aggregations, particularly during the winter full moon, when they gather for spawning. This mass spawning event is a sight to behold and is among the most remarkable natural spectacles in the Caribbean Sea.

Unfortunately, the Nassau Grouper's predictable spawning behavior, combined with its slow growth and late sexual maturation, makes it highly vulnerable to overfishing. This fact has led the International Union for Conservation of Nature (IUCN) to classify the Nassau Grouper as an endangered species.

Efforts are underway to conserve this captivating species. These include establishing marine protected areas, imposing fishing restrictions, particularly during spawning season, and educating the public about the importance of the Nassau Grouper to the Caribbean's marine ecosystem.

The Nassau Grouper is more than just a fascinating marine creature. It's a symbol of the Caribbean's rich biodiversity and a living testament to the intricate dance of evolution. In its charming stripes and captivating behavior, we are reminded of nature's creativity and the necessity of preserving the world's delicate marine ecosystems for future generations to admire and explore.

The Bountiful Butterflyfish

Butterflyfish are the vibrant jewels of the ocean. Enchanting scuba divers and marine biologists alike, their splendor brightens up the underwater realm with hues as diverse as the species themselves. Among this kaleidoscopic family, more than 120 species exist, each contributing to the vibrant tapestry of the marine world.

Butterflyfish, hailing from the family Chaetodontidae, are largely found in the warm, tropical waters of the Atlantic, Indian, and Pacific Oceans. However, for this chapter, we focus particularly on the species native to the Caribbean Sea. These include the Spotfin Butterflyfish, the Banded Butterflyfish, and the Four-eye Butterflyfish, all distinguished by their own unique patterns and behaviours.

Physically, butterflyfish possess a disc-like, laterally flattened body structure that is both fascinating and functional. Their size typically ranges from 4 to 8 inches, though some species can grow to around 12 inches. A hallmark feature of this family is the brightly coloured and distinctly patterned bodies, which are often a combination of yellow, white, black, and orange hues, making them easily identifiable even by novice snorkelers or divers.

The head of the butterflyfish features another distinguishing trait – a pointed snout. This elongated, narrow snout, equipped with small, brush-like teeth, has been a key factor in the dietary habits of these species, allowing them to access crevices in corals and rocks to feed on their preferred diet of invertebrates, coral polyps, and algae.

Butterflyfish are primarily diurnal creatures, meaning they are active during the day and rest at night. This is when their unique coloration plays a critical role in their survival. At night, many butterflyfish species can alter their colouration and patterns to a more subdued tone, making them less conspicuous to predators.

Socially, butterflyfish display fascinating behaviours. While some species live in small schools, many form monogamous pairs, which often remain together for life. These dedicated pairs are a delightful sight as they synchronously flit through coral reefs, adding a touch of romance to the marine world.

When it comes to breeding, many butterflyfish species engage in pelagic spawning – releasing their eggs into the water column. These eggs float freely, carried by the ocean currents until they hatch. The emerging larvae, known as tholichthys, are unique in their own right, possessing bony plates over their bodies which disappear as they mature.

The relationship between butterflyfish and coral reefs extends beyond the aesthetic. They are often considered indicators of reef health due to their reliance on coral for both food and shelter. Consequently, the decline in butterflyfish populations can signify deteriorating reef conditions.

Despite their visual appeal and ecological significance, butterflyfish face numerous threats. Coral reef degradation, primarily due to climate change and pollution, affects their habitat and food source. Overfishing and the aquarium trade also contribute to their dwindling numbers. Hence, the protection of butterflyfish calls for broader conservation measures that ensure the health of coral reefs and regulate marine trade.

In summary, the butterflyfish, with its rich variety and vibrant charm, is a testament to nature's artistic prowess. Its presence is woven into the delicate balance of the coral ecosystem, highlighting the intricate interplay between different marine organisms. In understanding and preserving these bountiful creatures, we take a step towards safeguarding the complexity and beauty of our oceanic world.

The Swimming Pigs of the Bahamas

Perhaps one of the most unusual sights in the Caribbean, a scene that at first might seem a part of an animated movie, is the unique spectacle of the swimming pigs in the Bahamas. As surprising as it might sound, these pigs have not only adapted to life on the sandy beaches but have also taken to the azure Caribbean waters with a gusto that's fascinating and delightful in equal measure.

Situated in the Exumas, a collection of 365 cays and islands in the Bahamas, is Pig Beach (officially known as Big Major Cay), the homeland of these extraordinary pigs. It is here that these free-roaming, aquatic porcine residents have become an endearing and popular attraction, drawing a steady stream of curious visitors from around the globe.

The pigs' origins are shrouded in a fair share of mystery and intrigue. While some theories suggest that the pigs were left on the island by sailors who intended to return but never did, others propose that the pigs are the survivors of a shipwreck. Yet another theory suggests that they were deliberately introduced to boost tourism. Regardless of how they first arrived, these pigs have settled into their beachfront lifestyle with evident enthusiasm.

Around 20 pigs and piglets make their home on Big Major Cay, frolicking in the warm, clear waters and lounging on the white sandy beaches. Despite being wild animals, these pigs have grown used to human interaction. They've learned that the sight of approaching boats often means incoming food, and they have become adept swimmers, paddling out to meet the visitors in hopes of a tasty snack.

The pigs are excellent swimmers, and their diet primarily consists of the food brought by tourists. They are omnivores by nature and have been observed eating a variety of fruits, vegetables, and even small amounts of meat. It's important to note, however, that while these pigs are relatively friendly and have grown accustomed to human presence, they are still wild animals, and their feeding is regulated to maintain their health and ensure the sustainability of their unique lifestyle.

Visiting the swimming pigs of the Bahamas provides a unique opportunity to observe these animals in an environment vastly different from what one would expect. The image of these plump, jovial creatures paddling through the turquoise waters, their snouts pointed eagerly towards incoming boats, has a certain surreal charm.

However, beyond the novelty and amusement, these pigs represent an interesting case of adaptation. They are a testament to the resilience and versatility of nature, demonstrating how animals can thrive in unexpected environments and forge unique relationships with humans.

While the swimming pigs of the Bahamas are indeed a delightful spectacle, they also emphasize the importance of responsible tourism. It's crucial for visitors to treat these unique creatures with respect, adhering to the guidelines for feeding and interaction. With the right balance of admiration and respect, we can ensure that the swimming pigs continue to thrive and delight visitors for many more years to come.

In the grand tapestry of Caribbean wildlife, the swimming pigs of the Bahamas have etched out a place of their own. They serve as a reminder of the endless surprises that nature holds and the joy that these surprises bring into our lives. They are indeed a sight to behold, an unanticipated harmony of nature and levity, set against the backdrop of the stunning Bahamian seascape.

Epilogue

As we close the pages on this detailed journey through the Caribbean's rich tapestry of wildlife, we take with us not only the vivid imagery of diverse species but also an understanding of their intrinsic roles in the ecosystems they inhabit.

We've soared alongside the stately Caribbean Brown Pelican, delved into the aquatic world of the Antillean Manatee, and marveled at the flashy Caribbean King Crab. These creatures, along with countless others, are integral threads in the fabric of life that clothe the islands.

We've delved into the struggles of endangered species, like the Jamaican Iguana, that teeter on the brink of extinction. Their plight is a solemn reminder of the crucial role of conservation in preserving our planet's biodiversity. We must continue to work towards a future where every species, regardless of its perceived value, is allowed to thrive in its natural habitat.

We've also witnessed the wonders of evolution and adaptation. The swimming pigs of the Bahamas, in particular, stand as testament to the wonders of the natural world. Their unique ability to swim in the Caribbean seas, while being pigs, underscores the enduring adaptability and resilience of life. They, among other extraordinary creatures, like Caribbean Lampreys, speak to the myriad ways in which life forms can adapt and prosper in diverse environments.

Equally important are the ecosystems that host this wide array of life. The vibrant coral reefs, deep blue seas, lush mangroves, sandy beaches, and dense forests of the Caribbean are more than just habitats. They are life-supporting matrices that provide food, shelter, and breeding grounds for countless species. They're a reminder of the delicate balance that exists between every organism and its environment, a harmony that is as beautiful as it is complex.

This journey has taken us beyond the surface to unveil the Caribbean's hidden biological treasures. Each creature, big or small, plays a vital role in shaping the environment and influencing other species around it. They are all interconnected in the great circle of life, contributing to the intricate and delicate balance of their ecosystems.

In the end, this exploration of the Caribbean's wildlife is more than just a study of individual species. It is a celebration of biodiversity, a call to conservation, and a tribute to the intricate dance of life that unfolds across our planet. As we contemplate the mysteries and marvels of the natural world, let us strive to respect and preserve the environments that sustain it.

As we end our journey, it's crucial to remember that every creature we've encountered, from the smallest frogs to the largest manatee, contributes invaluably to the biodiversity of the planet. The beauty of the natural world lies in its diversity, and in the complex interplay of species that contribute to the dynamic balance of life. As stewards of the Earth, it is our responsibility to ensure the continuation of this grand, intricate tapestry of life. Let this book serve as a beacon of awareness and understanding, illuminating the richness of the Caribbean wildlife, and inspiring respect and compassion for all creatures that share our planet.

In preserving them, we are, in essence, preserving ourselves. It's a relationship defined by coexistence and mutual respect, and the key to this is in our hands. As we look to the future, we carry with us the hope that our efforts today will ensure the survival and prosperity of these incredible species for generations to come.

Printed in Great Britain
by Amazon

32806453R00066